Dedication

I would like to dedicate this book to my wife Debbie and daughter Kimberley for all their persistence to guide me in this endeavor and to look forward to future ones.

Acknowledgments

I have a few people that I must thank because without their technical experience and their friendship, this book would not have been possible.

My wife, Debbie, has been extremely helpful in the printing and compiling of information, and in helping me understand just how a computer really works. For this I have come to appreciate her abilities.

I would like to thank Serena Landis for her magnificent photography and her professional approach to helping me in this project. Without her help I feel the project would have not been completed.

My parents probably don't realize it, but without their enthusiasm in my artistic abilities as I was growing up I probably would not have pursued this project at this time in my life.

Last, but not least I want to thank our Creator for giving us the ability to express ourselves in so many artistic adventures.

© 1999, 2012 by Randy True

Written & illustrated by Randy True
Photographs by Serena Landis

ISBN 978-1-56523-751-3

Library of Congress Cataloging-in-Publication Data

True, Randy.
Whittling pencils / Randy True.
    p. cm.
Originally published: Pencil carving / Randy True. 1999.
ISBN 978-1-56523-751-3
1. Wood-carving. 2. Pencils. I. Title. II. Title: Pencil carving.
TT199.7.T795 2012
745.51--dc23
        2012017077

To learn more about the other great books from Fox Chapel Publishing, or to find a retailer near you, call toll-free 800-457-9112 or visit us at *www.FoxChapelPublishing.com*.

Note to Authors: We are always looking for talented authors to write new books. Please send a brief letter describing your idea to Acquisition Editor, 1970 Broad Street, East Petersburg, PA 17520.

Printed in China
First printing

Introduction

I have been intrigued since the first time I saw a carved pencil at a show I was attending and thought, "What a great idea, yet, it's so small! How did they do that?"

Through one of the carving clubs I now belong to, a class was set up for pencil carving. I thought, great, but what should I expect? What are we going to carve on it?

I soon learned you don't use your regular, larger carving tools, nor do you carve on a regular pencil. Oh, you can carve on one of the oversized wooden pencils, but let's face it, the wood used in a pencil wasn't meant for carving.

The pencils I carve, like most oversized pencils sold, are made of a resin or plastic, if you will. This type is much easier to carve and holds detail quite well.

As for the tools, micro carving tools seem to work very well. And be sure to have plenty of light to work by!

Well, let's get started!

Supplies

No woodworking project can begin without having the proper supplies on hand and the projects in this book are no exception to that rule.

TOOLS

- Regular, fine point detail knife
- ⅛" (3mm) straight gouge or comparable tool
- The following tools are micro-mini carving tools carried by your local carving tool suppliers and craft stores. Use a 1.5 or 2.0 mm size if possible. Larger tools increase the difficulty.
    - V-tool
    - U-gouge
    - Straight paring chisel
    - Optional: If available, a sheep's hook micro tool helps clean up the eye cuts, but this tool is not necessary.
- Important: Use a good carving glove for this project. It's a must! Carving on a round object is tricky and a carving glove sometimes cannot stop all cuts, even from small tools.

SUPPLIES

- Pencils—child's oversized or "first" pencil
- A couple of brands I have found that are good for this type of carving are Berol or Empire pencils. I'm sure there are others, but to ensure you are getting the resin or plastic type, look at the sharpened end. In a plastic or resin pencil, there are no seams where the pencil is formed around the lead. On wooden pencils you can see where the two halves are put together around the lead.
- Paints—acrylics
    - White
    - Orange
    - Red
    - (I also use an oil paint wash technique to antique the pencil after the acrylic painting is done.)
- Thinner or medium
- Copal—for a satin finish
- Pale drying oil—sets the finish for faster drying time
- Oil paint color—burnt umber
- Craft acrylic spray sealer—matte finish

Note: The author used these products for the projects in this book. Substitute your choice of brands, tools, and materials as desired.

Carving the Santa Pencil

Santa Claus is a favorite subject for virtually every type of
carving and woodworking that exists,
but he works particularly well for pencil carving.

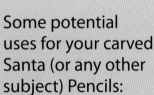

Some potential uses for your carved Santa (or any other subject) Pencils:

- As Christmas tree ornaments
- As part of the decorations on your Christmas presents
- As stocking stuffers
- As gifts for your child's teachers
- As sales items at craft fairs. They are real eye catchers
- As teaching tools for other members of your local woodcarving club

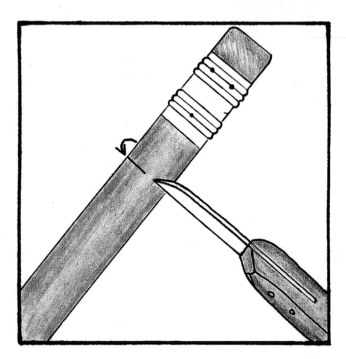

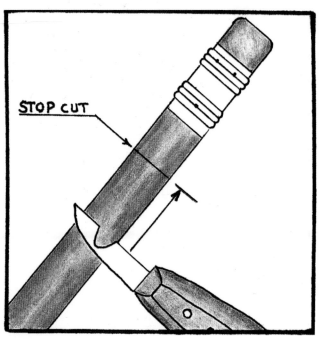

1 **Make a stop cut.**
Using a finishing knife, score or make a stop cut 360º around the pencil about ½" below the metal band.

2 **Remove the paint.**
Next, take the same knife and drop down the pencil about 1" or so and shave the paint off all the way around the pencil, back to the stop cut.

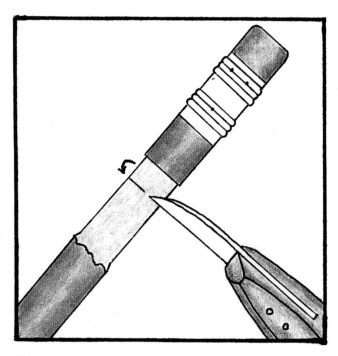

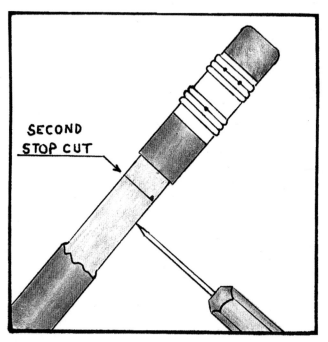

3 **Second stop cut.**
From that same stop cut, drop down ¼" and make another 360º stop cut.

4 **Use the chisel.**
Take the straight paring chisel and drop down about ¼" below the last stop cut and push the paring chisel straight in.

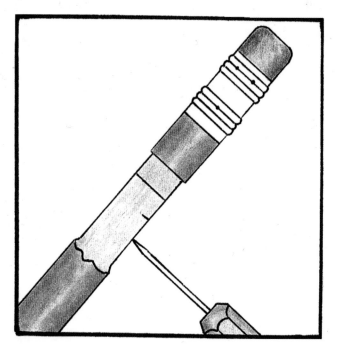

5 **Repeat the cut.**
Drop down another ¼" from that cut and repeat the same cut. Push in the chisel about ¹⁄₁₆" to ⅛". Be careful when making the cut.

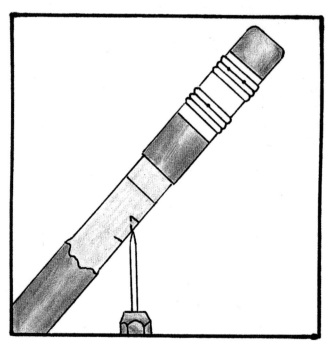

6 **Making nose cuts.**
With the paring chisel on the first cut of the bridge of the nose, take chisel and cut in from the top and bottom to the straight cut at a 45º angle.

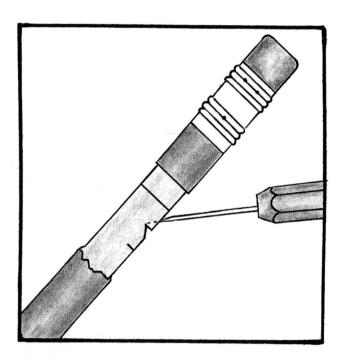

7 **The bridge.**
You have created the bridge of the nose.

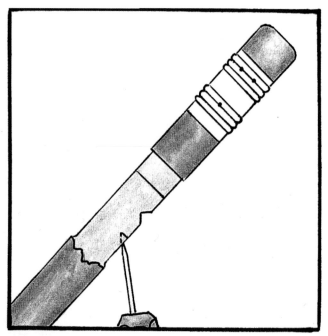

8 **More facial cuts.**
Continuing with the same chisel, move down to the second cut. Make another 45º cut from the bottom up to the stop cut. This will form the underneath part of the nose and mustache.

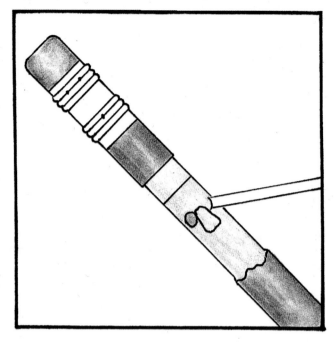

9 Form the nose.
With the V-tool, start making a triangular cut to form the nose. Make the nose larger than it ultimately will be—it can be reduced later.

10 Cut the eye sockets.
Take the 3mm straight gouge to cut out the eye sockets. Cut the sockets out at a slight downward angle. Make sockets about ⅛" deep. Make the left eye first, and then match the right eye to it.

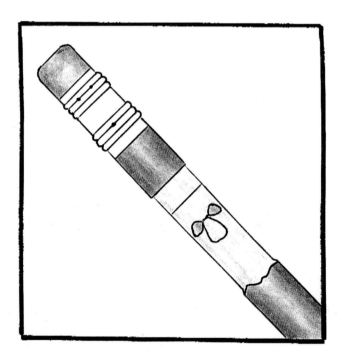

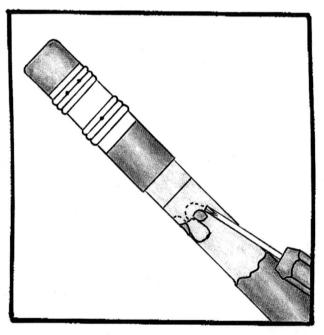

11 Stop and compare.
Stop and compare your pencil with the illustration. Your work should resemble the above.

12 Creating eyebrows.
Using the V-tool, start at the corner of the eye and outline the top line of the eyebrow on both sides to the bridge of the nose.

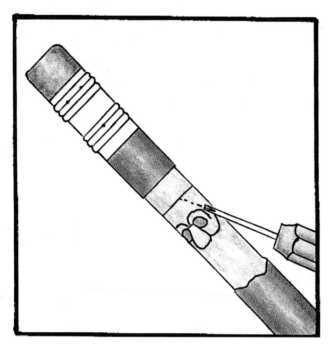

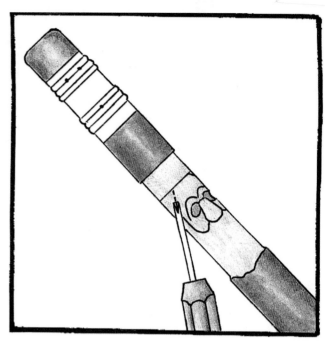

13 **Outlining the mustache and cheek.**
Still using the V-tool, start at the corner of the nose and cut a line up to and around the eyebrow, all the way to the stop cut of the hat. This will outline the mustache and cheek.

14 **Repeat the cut.**
Now repeat the same cut on the right side. Take your time and try to make both sides even.

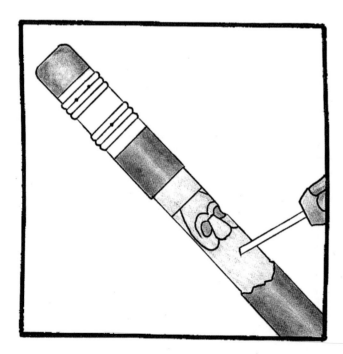

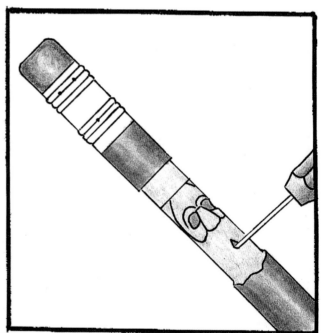

15 **Form the upper lip.**
Use the V-tool and drop down from your stop cut under the nose by about ¼" and push your V-tool upside down, straight in to form the upper lip. Be careful not to pry or you will break your V-tool!

16 **Form the mouth.**
Use the micro gouge and push straight in to form the lower lip. Repeat the previous step with the V-tool and then gouge again to get the piece to pop out, forming the mouth. Again, do not pry.

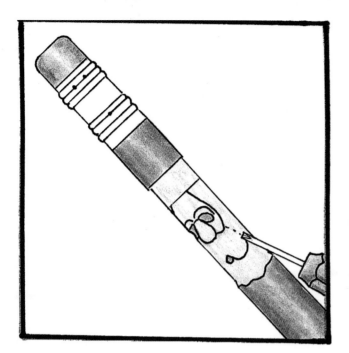

17 **Cutting a connection.**
Use the V-tool to cut a line from the corner of the mouth, sweeping upward to a point meeting the previous mustache/cheek cut. Make the connection along the line even with underneath side of nose.

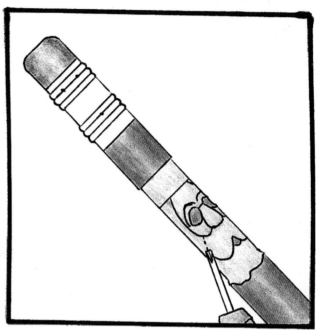

18 **Repeat.**
Repeat the process on the right side, making sure the sides mirror each other.

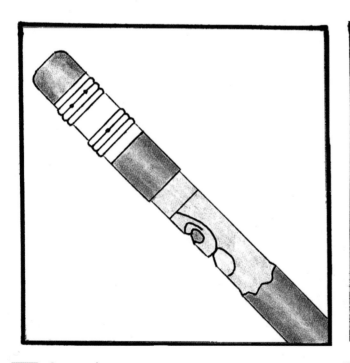

19 **Stop and compare.**
From a side view, this is what your project should resemble.

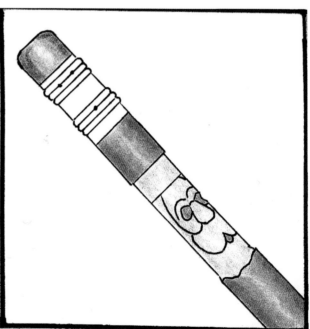

20 **From the front.**
From the front, your project should look similar to what you see above.

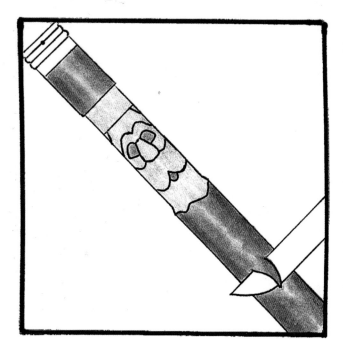

21 **Forming the beard.**
Before detailing the face, finish removing the paint from the pencil to form the beard. Taper down to a point and shave only deep enough with your finishing knife to remove the paint.

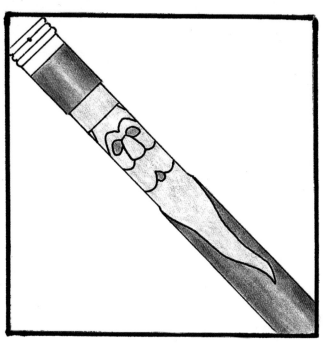

22 **Stop and compare.**
Your project should resemble the above front view. You may opt for further beard changes later.

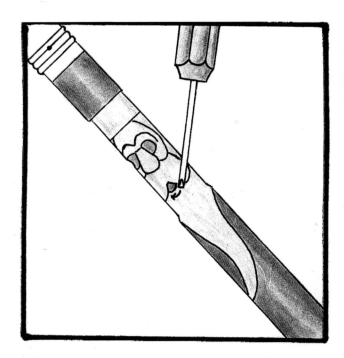

23 **Form the bottom lip.**
With your gouge, form the bottom lip by leaving a ridge after outlining the previous gouge cut.

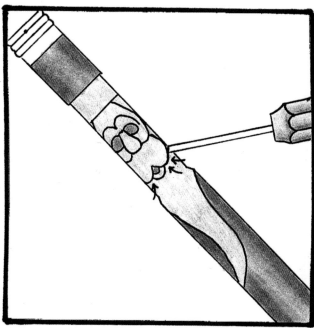

24 **Cutting the mustache.**
Now with the straight paring chisel you can begin to undercut the mustache.

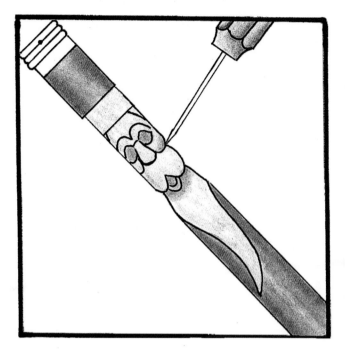

25 **Make a stop cut.**
Using the paring chisel, go back over the V-tool cuts on the mustache and make a stop cut.

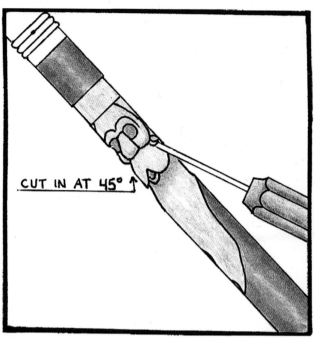

CUT IN AT 45°

26 **Highlight the mustache.**
Push the chisel in at a 45º angle to stop cut to help bring out and highlight the mustache.

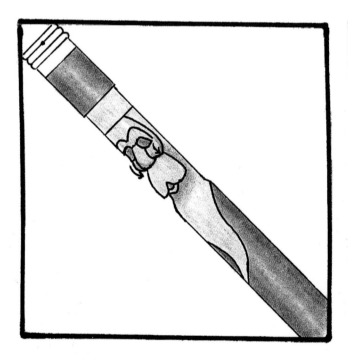

27 **Rounding the cheeks.**
Next, using the same chisel, proceed with the same process on the cheek using a stop cut and not a 45° cut. Round over to the stop cut to give Santa's cheeks a jolly look!

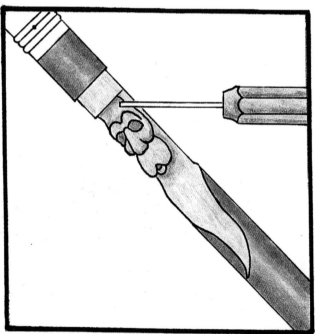

28 **Eyebrows, forehead, and temple.**
Using the paring chisel, work down the area around the eyebrows, forehead (if any left), and temples on the side.

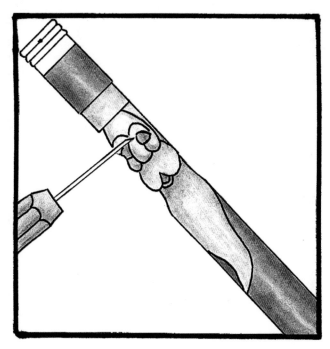

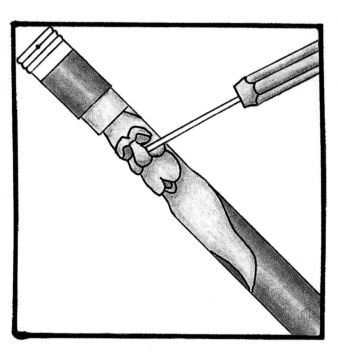

29 **Shaping the nose.**
Now, go back to the bridge of the nose with the paring chisel and go deeper with that stop cut; start shaping the nose and the sides of the nose.

30 **Giving the nose depth.**
Follow the outline of the nose with stop cuts and go deeper to bring depth to the nose as shown.

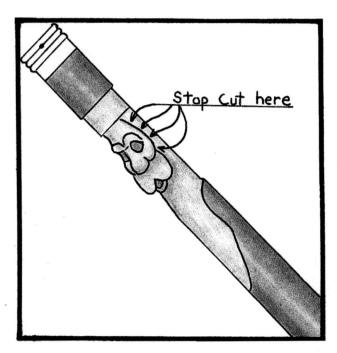

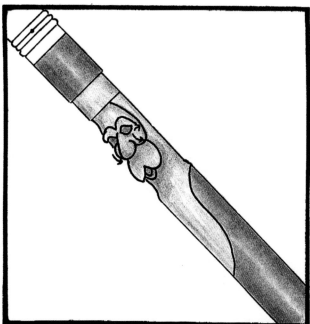

31 **More cheek rounding.**
Make stop cuts as shown above on the side, and round the cheek down to the stop cut.

32 **Work the cheeks.**
Work the cheeks down to make the nose stand out more. Try to keep the cheeks rounded.

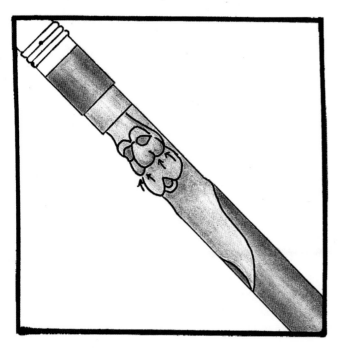

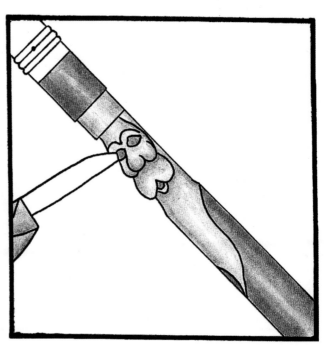

33 **Rounding the mustache.**
Take the paring chisel and round the mustache over to the stop cut for the cheek. This gives a more finished look to it.

34 **Chip cutting eye and socket.**
Carefully take the point of the finish knife and make a chip cut to form the eye and socket. Use a three-corner cut, just like a chip carving cut is made; it should pop out when properly done.

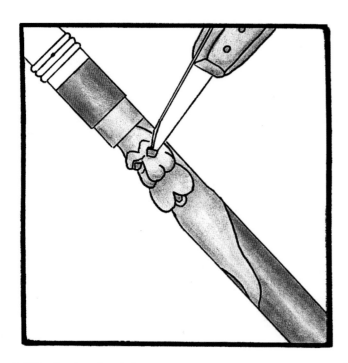

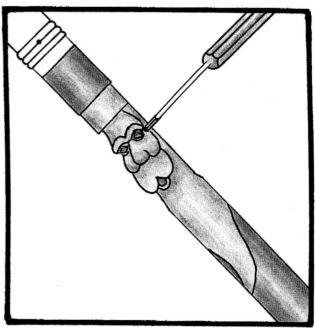

35 **Cutting the right eye.**
Make the same chip cut on the right eye. You will know it's deep enough when the pencil lead starts to show to form the dark spot of the eye.

36 **Creating the smile.**
With the V-tool, create crow's feet at the outside corner of the eye to create that smiling effect.

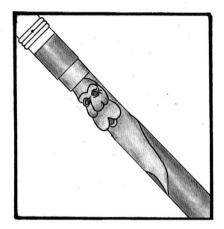

37 **Stop and compare.**
At this point, the carving should look like the drawing above. The outside corners of the eyebrows may need to be trimmed down. Use your own judgment.

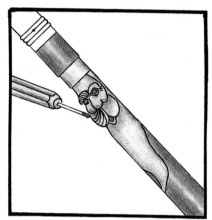

38 **Forming hair.**
Using the V-tool, start making cuts to form hair on the eyebrows and mustache. Use only the very point of the V-tool for best results. Don't go too deep.

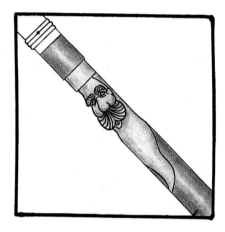

39 **Compare again**
At this stage, the project should resemble the above.

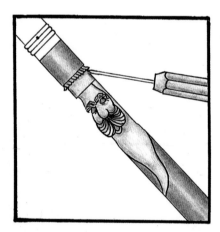

40 **Create the fur.**
Next, use the paring chisel to make the fur around the edge of the cap. Take the chisel, cut in at a 45° angle and lift slightly. Go all the way around, making rows of these (usually three rows).

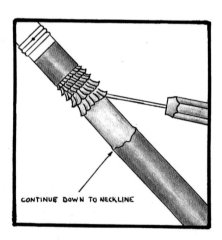

CONTINUE DOWN TO NECKLINE

41 **Back of the head.**
Using the micro gouge on the back of the head, apply the same technique, but stagger your cuts, as with shingles on a roof. Let the pieces curl up slightly, but try not to break them off.

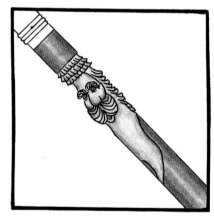

42 **Stop and compare.**
This is how your carving should look from the front. This piece is now ready for the beard to be finished. See "Beard Variations" beginning on page 28.

Carving the Wood Spirit Pencil

In carving the Wood Spirit Pencil, I wanted to try and keep the mystical look to it. I wanted to have the long flowing beard and also the wind blown hair look.

I also carved the eyebrows with a more serious look to them.

The Wood Spirit is probably carved as much as any subject by woodcarvers than anything else. Now we can even carve them in pencils, too.

1 Creating a face.
Using the knife, make an oval shape for the face by shaving off the paint starting about 1" below the metal band and continuing about another 1" down. Shave about halfway around for the width of the face.

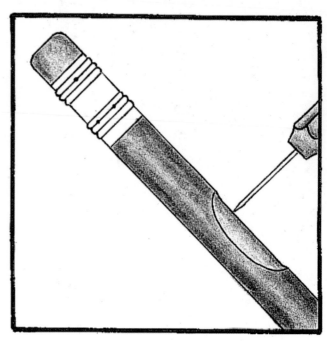

2 Bridge of nose.
Measure ¼" down from the top of the oval, use the paring chisel straight in for the bridge of the nose.

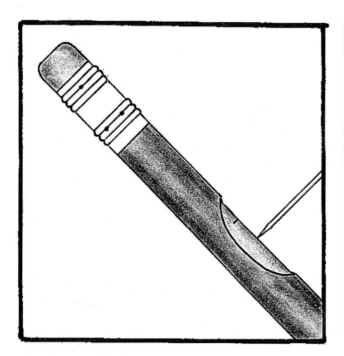

3 Nose cut.
Drop down ¼" from that cut, and again using the paring chisel, go straight in again.

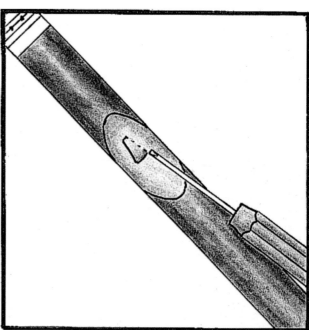

4 Nose triangle.
Using the V-tool, make the triangular shape for the nose but keep it a little narrower than the Santa nose. Refer to steps 6 through 9 of the Santa Pencil section.

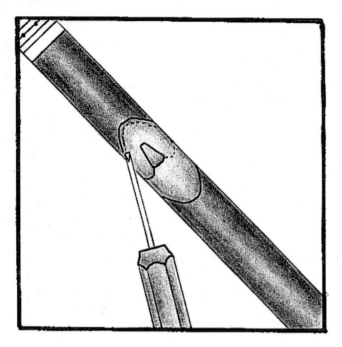

5 **Facial line.**
With the V-tool, start at the corner of the nose and circle around to meet on the other corner of the nose.

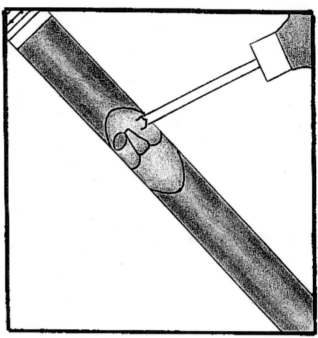

6 **Cutting the eye sockets.**
Using the 3mm palm gouge, create eye sockets as before on both sides.

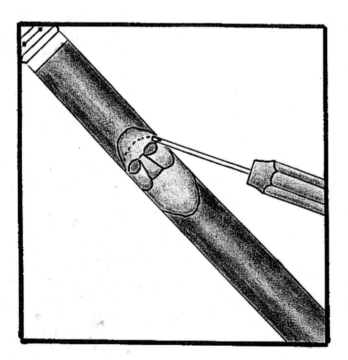

7 **Eyebrows.**
Using the V-tool again, outline both sides of the eyebrows.

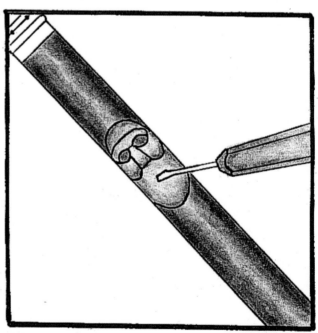

8 **Upper mouth.**
Measure about ⅛" below the bottom of the nose and take the micro V-tool upside down and push straight in to form the upper part of the mouth.

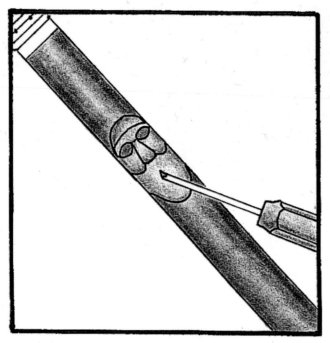

9 **Lower mouth.**
Take the micro U-gouge and, at a slight angle, push in to form the bottom of the mouth. We are going to make the mouth appear to be opened wider than in the Santa Pencil.

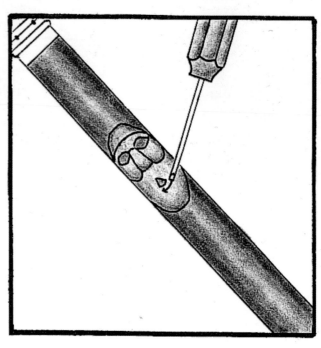

10 **Bottom lip.**
Still using the micro gouge, run under the mark just made to form the bottom lip.

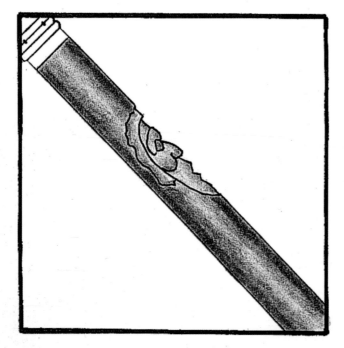

11 **Creating hair.**
Take your knife and remove paint for the hair on both sides of the face and above the head about ⅛" past the V-tool cut that formed the face.

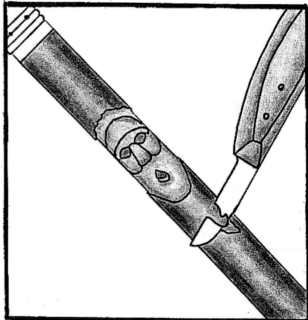

12 **Creating the beard.**
With the knife, remove more paint from the pencil to form the beard. Use a sweeping motion to achieve a flowing beard.

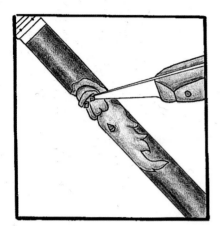

13 **Cutting the eyes.**
Before beginning the cut-ins for the beard, use chip cuts to form the eyes, as in step 34 of the Santa Pencil Project.

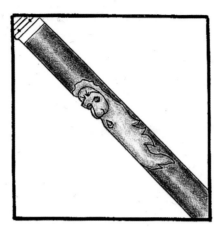

14 **Serious eyebrows.**
Using the V-tool, make cuts to create a serious look for the eyebrows.

15 **Crow's feet and wrinkles.**
Using the same V-tool, make crow's feet for the corners of the eyes and wrinkles on the forehead.

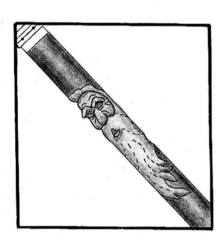

16 **Beard layers.**
Using the micro V-tool, make deep cuts on the beard to form high and low layers. Be certain to make flowing cuts.

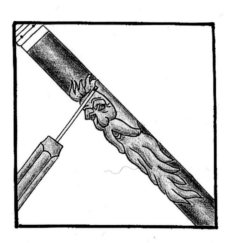

17 **Hair cuts.**
On the side of the face where the beard starts, take the micro V-tool and make moderate sweeping cuts for hair. Let the V-tool go just past where you shaved off paint to accent the flow of the hair.

18 **Completing.**
Continue making sweeping V-tool cuts on the rest of the beard and mustache. Your Wood Spirit Pencil is now complete.

Carving the Uncle Sam Pencil

In carving this Uncle Sam Pencil we will go through some familiar steps from carving the Santa Pencil. I will from time to time refer to certain steps in the chapter "Carving the Santa Pencil" in order to simplify my procedure in carving the Uncle Sam Pencil.

I hope you enjoy this one because it was fun creating this patriotic carved pencil. Also at the end of this chapter I have created a few more variations that you may want to try. Well, let's get patriotic and see if we can carve an Uncle Sam just for you!

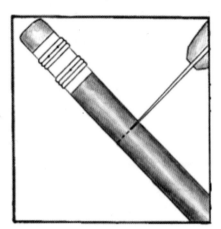

1 **Start with a stop cut.**
Start with a stop cut 1" below the metal band on the pencil. Continue the stop cut 360° around the pencil.

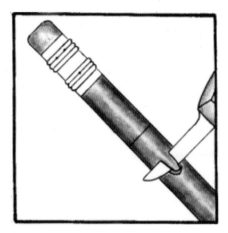

2 **Shaving the pencil.**
Next move about ¾" down and shave paint off up to stop cut 360° around the pencil.

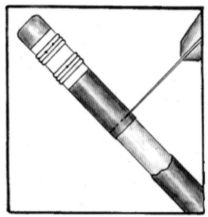

3 **Second stop cut.**
Now, going back to our first stop cut, proceed to move up ⅛" and make another stop cut.

4 **A third stop cut.**
Still working on the hat, go up another ½" and make another stop cut here.

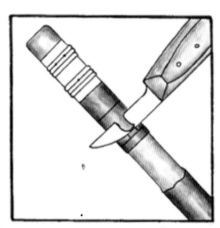

5 **Shave the paint.**
Using the knife, shave off the paint between these last two stop cuts on the hat.

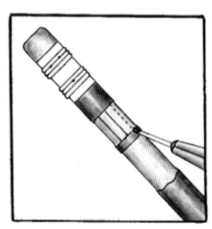

6 **Vertical stripes.**
Use the micro V-tool and make vertical cuts for the stripes about ⅛" apart on the hat. Make sure vertical sections add up to alternate red and white color striping.

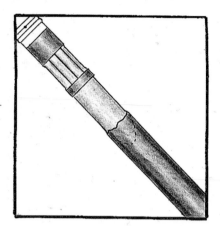

7 **Select the front.**
Pick which side will be the front of the pencil. Take the knife and shave down about ⅜" to make the beard come to a rounded point, as shown.

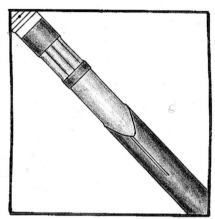

8 **Begin the vest.**
Where the rounded point of the beard ends, use the V-tool and make the first vertical cut for Uncle Sam's vest about ¾" long. Make the cut left of center, as shown, about ¹⁄₁₆".

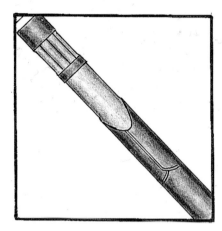

9 **Overlapping cuts.**
Still using the V-tool, make overlapping cuts for the bottom of the vest outward where it meets the long-tailed overcoat.

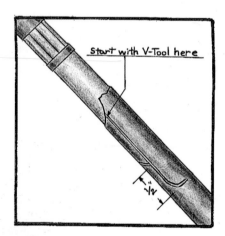

Start with V-Tool here

½"

10 **Overcoat cuts.**
Looking at one side, make the overcoat cuts beside the vest from the beard down to where the coattails begin. The cuts go beyond the bottom of the vest, about ½" before making the tail cuts.

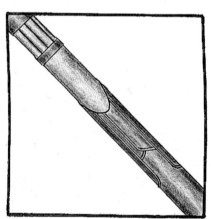

11 **Repeat.**
Repeat the cut for the other side before cutting in the tail of the overcoat. Your work should look like the above.

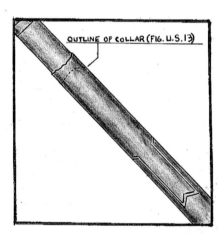

OUTLINE OF COLLAR (FIG. U.S.13)

12 **Cutting the tail.**
Turn the pencil around to the back and use the V-tool to cut the tail in, going about 1" long before making an upside-down V for the bottom of the tail.

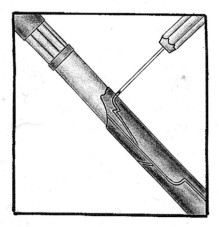

13 **Lapel cutting.**
Look at one side of the overcoat and use the V-tool to cut in the lapel as shown. Repeat this step on the other side, and make a cut to form the collar in the back.

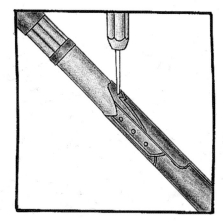

14 **Relief-style buttons.**
Returning to the vest, use the micro gouge and make buttons on the front of the vest and on the corners of the lapel as shown. To make buttons, push the gouge straight in, make a circle, and then remove the piece for a relief-style button.

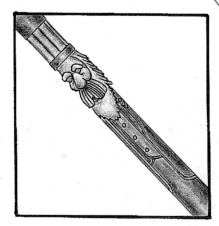

15 **Carve the face.**
Next, carve the face. Refer back to steps 4 through 41 in the Santa Pencil section. Leave out steps that relate to carving the fur on the hat. When doing the mustache on the Uncle Sam, use the V-tool and make hair lines as shown here.

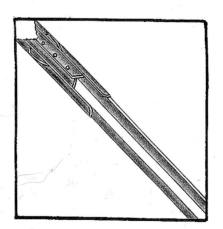

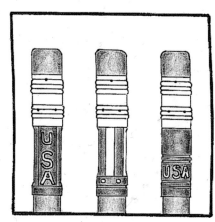

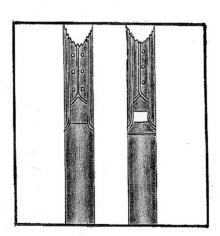

16 **Alternative styles.**
Here are some alternative styles for the barrel of your Uncle Sam Pencil.

Carving the Leprechaun Pencil

In carving the Leprechaun Pencil you will find some similarities to that of the Uncle Sam Pencil.

The Leprechaun Pencil is the result of me receiving requests for pencils celebrating different holidays during the year. I have been trying new ideas and this one has only a few variations.

I hope you enjoy carving it as much as I have.

Let's see if we can bring out the Irish in this pencil!

Variations.

Unlike some of the other pencil carving subjects, The Leprechaun has but a few variations, including with and without a mustache.

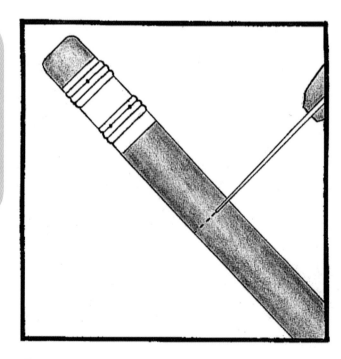

1 **First stop cut.**
Using the knife, make a stop cut about 1" below the metal band.

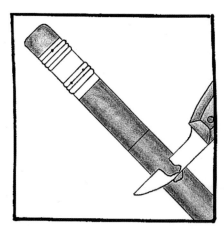

2 **Remove paint.**
Drop down from the stop cut ¾" and shave paint off back up to your stop cut. Be sure to do it all the way around the pencil.

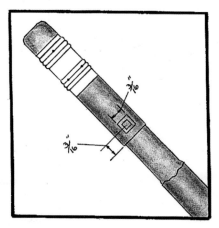

3 **Create the buckle.**
Using the V-tool, make a buckle on the hat about ³⁄₁₆" square, leaving ³⁄₁₆" to the center of buckle from the first stop cut.

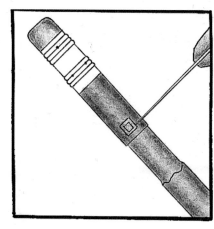

4 **Hatband.**
Using the knife, make the hatband. Make the first line ⅛" up from the stop cut.

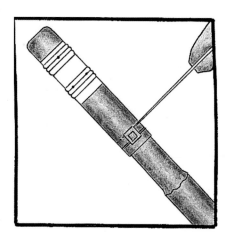

5 **Second hatband line.**
Move up another ⅛" for the final line on the hatband. After this, go over these last two steps with the V-tool to cut in for painting.

6 **Shamrock.**
Use either the V-tool or a power carving tool to outline a shamrock on the hat, just above the buckle.

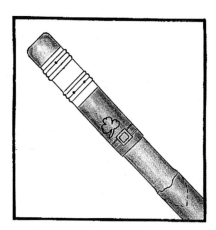

7 **Front established.**
The hat establishes the front of the carving, so you can now carve the beard down, as we did with step 7 of the Uncle Sam Project.

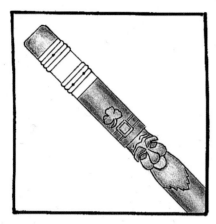

8 **No mustache.**
In carving the Leprechaun face, eliminate the mustache. Use the steps as before to carve the face and make the upper lip out of what would be the mustache.

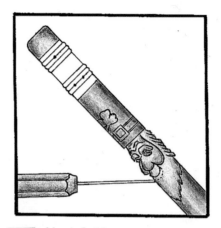

9 **Lip definition.**
Where the lips meet, use the V-tool to help define the area.

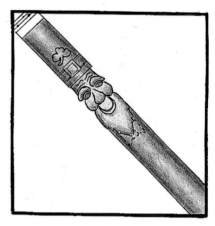

10 **Jacket and bowtie.**
The Leprechaun's jacket is double-breasted, and he wears a bowtie. Use the V-tool and make an outline for both under the beard.

11 **Vertical cuts.**
Using the V-tool, make vertical cuts about 1" long centered up with the bow tie.

12 **Buttons.**
Using the micro-gouge, we will make buttons on each side of the center of the vest. Usually about three sets are all you will have room for.

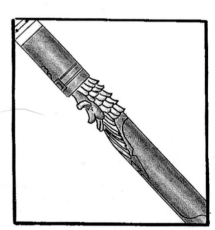

13 **Narrow and pointed nose.**
In creating the Leprechaun, the nose is more narrow and pointed than for the Santa Claus or Uncle Sam projects.

14 **Alternative styles.**
In this version I've left the mustache and beard, and have painted them orange.

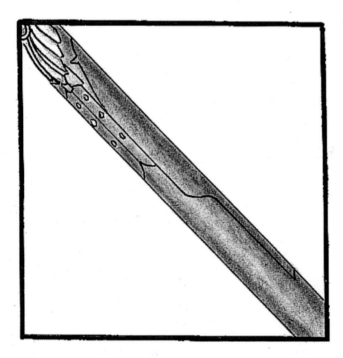

15 **Completing.**
To complete the carving, use the same steps for the overcoat in the Uncle Sam Pencil, steps 10–14.

Beard Variations

There are three basic styles of beard used for the projects in this book. Use different ones for the same project and see if you like the results and which one you like to carve best.

From left to right: Layered, Sweeping, Spiral

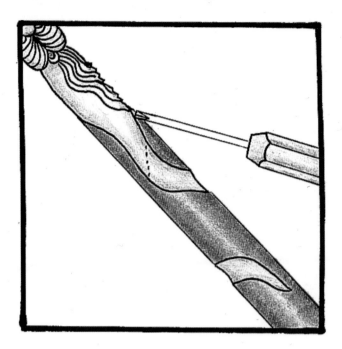

Spiral beard.

The spiral style seems to be the most popular. When shaving paint off to where the beard comes to a point in the first step, just continue from there around one revolution and end back in front, aligned with the face. Then add hair in the wavy pattern all the way around the spiral part of the beard with the V-tool.

Sweeping beard.

Use the micro V-tool for the sweeping beard style. Start under the lip with the V-tool and make sweeping cuts from there to the left and right of the center. Then start at the outer edge and work to the center on the long part of the beard so that both sides meet in the center to form an upside-down V. Continue down to the tip of the beard.

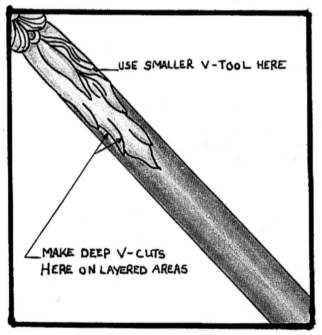

USE SMALLER V-TOOL HERE

MAKE DEEP V-CUTS HERE ON LAYERED AREAS

Layered beard.

Create the layered beard style by making deep V-cuts with the finish knife, removing the pieces, and then proceeding with the V-tool to carve hair for the beard.

Painting and Finishing

How you paint and finish your carved pencil is as important as how you carve it. There are some rules to follow and some tricks you can borrow to create pencils that anyone would be thrilled to receive.

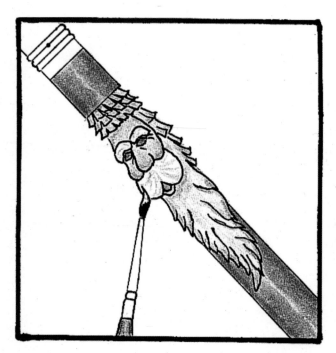

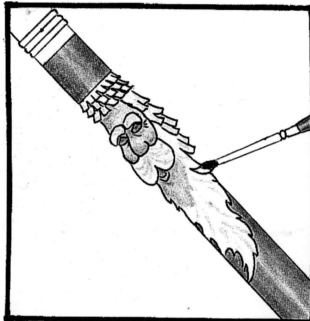

Full strength.
When painting your Santa Pencil, start with white acrylic paint at full strength on the eyebrows and mustache. I find a 000 paint brush works well on these pencils.

Reduced strength.
Next, using white paint on the brush along with a slight bit of water, continue to paint the hair, beard, and fur on the brim of the cap.

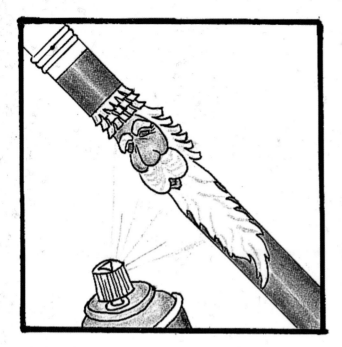

Seal acrylic paint.
Before beginning the antique wash process, first seal the white acrylic paint to keep from picking up too much of the oil paint when staining. Use a craft acrylic spray sealer and spray the entire pencil. Dry thoroughly before proceeding.

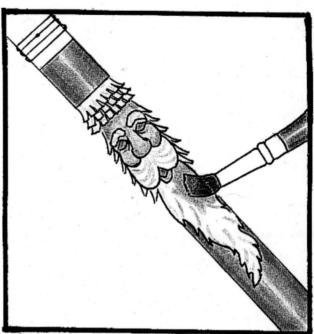

Applying stain.
Combine a mixture of 15 drops of paint thinner, 2 drops of copal, 2 drops of pale drying oil, and 1 part burnt umber. Using a stout, short-haired brush, thoroughly brush the stain in all painted areas as well as the facial area (eyes, hair, etc.). Let stand about 30 seconds and then wipe clean with a cloth to your liking.

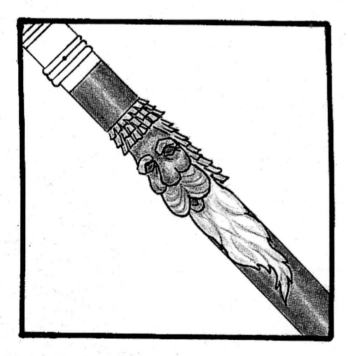

Stop and compare.
Compare your work with the one above. Notice the stain brings out all the detail in the beard, hair, mustache, and even the crow's feet around the eyes. Also, no sealer is required over the stain because the copal added to your mixture seals it.

Tip.

When painting the V-tool markings for overcoats on the Uncle Sam and Leprechaun pencils, take a 000 paint brush with white acrylic paint and go over all V-tool cuts. When the paint begins to dry, take the edge of your fingernail and scrape the excess off to make crisp V-tool lines.

Author Randy True

About the Author

I was born in what is known as Middletown, U.S.A., or as most of us call it, Muncie, Indiana. Growing up around the farming community and auto industry, the artistic part of me was there but not brought forth as it is now. I always enjoyed sketching and some painting, but it really wasn't quite a passion yet.

Like most men, I've always wanted to build things and be somewhat creative. My interest turned toward cabinet and furniture making. Soon I realized that it was satisfying, but there was still the artistic part that was missing.

Talking to a friend who is a shop instructor, I was told of a woodcarving club. One thing has led to another and I have found the artistic release I needed.

I have joined some local woodcarving clubs to help further my knowledge in the endeavor, and have found woodcarvers to be the most helpful and sincere people around.

Because of my love for this form of art, I am looking forward to helping others get started and hope to pursue a career in the art of wood sculpture.

My family has and always will be my inspiration in all areas of life. They have been there with advice when needed and that extra push when I doubted myself.

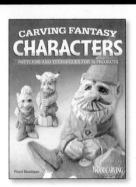

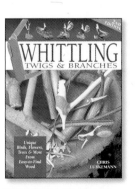